Jake and Quin

by Calvin Baker
illustrated by Tim O'Connor

Decodable 26

Mc Graw Hill Education

Bothell, WA • Chicago, IL • Columbus, OH • New York, NY

MHEonline.com

Send all inquiries to:
McGraw-Hill Education
8787 Orion Place
Columbus, OH 43240

ISBN: 978-0-02-132414-9
MHID: 0-02-132414-X

Printed in China

10 11 12 13 14 DSS 28 27 26 25 24

Quin and Jake were cute cats.

Can cats make some fun?

Rope Fun

Quin tugs a rope as Jake tugs.
Then Jake quits.

Quin drops in some mud, but not Jake.
Jake helps Quin up.

Fun at Bat

Jake bats.
Jake runs as Quin claps.
Then Quin bats.

Quin uses a big bat, but he cannot hit!

Quin kept at it.

Quin can hit!
Jake claps.
Jake and Quin were fun cats!